AF291214

With thanks to Dr Carrie Soderman, Department of Earth Sciences,
and further advice from Dr Sally Collins and Amy Barker at the
Sedgwick Museum of Earth Sciences, University of Cambridge.

First published 2026 by Nosy Crow Ltd
Wheat Wharf, 27a Shad Thames,
London, SE1 2XZ, UK

Nosy Crow Eireann Ltd
c/o Fieldfisher Ireland LLP
45 Mespil Road, Dublin 4,
D04 W2F1, Ireland

ISBN 9781805133285 (HB)
ISBN 9781805133292 (PB)

Nosy Crow and associated logos are trademarks
and/or registered trademarks of Nosy Crow Ltd.

Text © Tamsin Mather and David Pyle 2026
Illustrations © Daniel Long 2026

Published in collaboration with the University of Cambridge

The rights of Tamsin Mather and David Pyle to be identified as the authors
and Daniel Long to be identified as the illustrator of this work has been asserted.
All rights reserved.

This book is sold subject to the condition that it shall not,
by way of trade or otherwise, be lent, hired out or otherwise circulated in
any form of binding or cover other than that in which it is published.
No part of this publication may be reproduced, stored in a retrieval system,
or transmitted in any form or by any means
(electronic, mechanical, photocopying, recording or otherwise)
without the prior written permission of Nosy Crow Ltd.

The publisher and copyright holders prohibit the use of either text or illustrations to develop any
generative machine learning artificial intelligence (AI) models or related technologies.

A CIP catalogue record for this book is available from the British Library.

Printed in China following rigorous ethical sourcing standards.

10 9 8 7 6 5 4 3 2 1 (HB)
10 9 8 7 6 5 4 3 2 1 (PB)

THE POWER OF VOLCANOES

written by
TAMSIN MATHER and DAVID PYLE

illustrated by
DANIEL LONG

Contents

Introduction

Volcanoes make some of the most amazing landscapes on Earth. Some are always active, glowing red at night and fuming by day. Others only explode or erupt every few hundred or thousand years and are completely quiet in between.

Volcanic eruptions can be devastating and have buried entire cities, but they also create land and are part of what keeps our planet alive. As we have reached out into space, we have found volcanoes on other worlds, some of them spectacularly active . . . and we are still finding out new things about volcanoes every day! Read on to discover the science behind volcanoes, how we study them and what makes them the most incredible places on our planet.

Perhaps one day you too will uncover some of their secrets . . .

—TAMSIN MATHER and DAVID PYLE

What is a volcano?

You might have seen volcanoes on TV, in films or on the internet,
erupting spectacularly with dark, billowing ash clouds.
But what actually is a volcano?

Our planet, Earth, is made up of several different layers.
The top layer, known as the **crust**, is the thinnest and coolest
layer. This is what we live on! It is made of solid rock.

Two-thirds of Earth's surface
is covered by seas and
oceans. That means most of
Earth's crust is underwater.

Below the crust is the **mantle**,
Earth's largest layer. Here, the
solid rock is so hot that it behaves
like a sticky liquid, moving or
creeping really slowly.

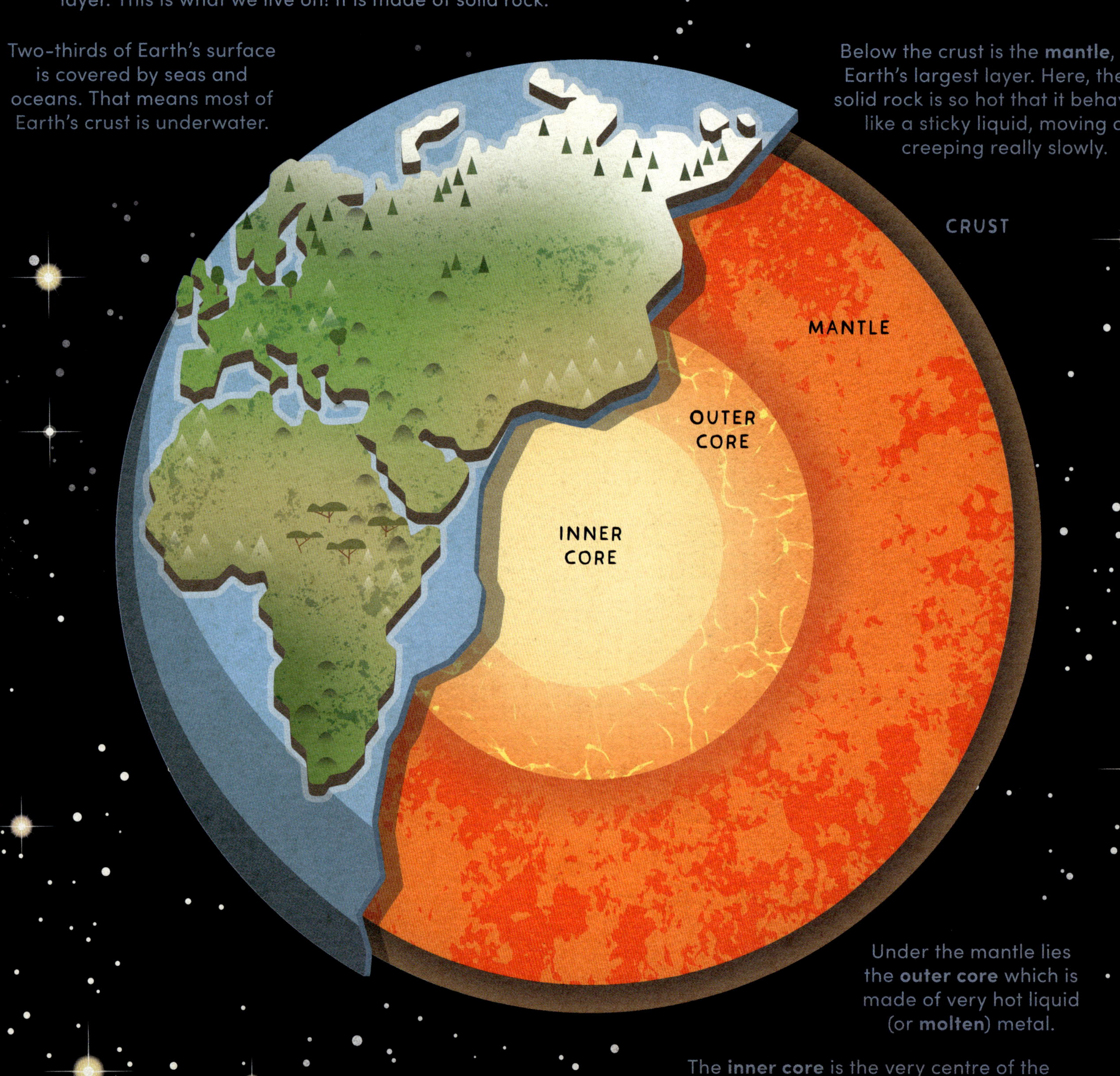

Under the mantle lies
the **outer core** which is
made of very hot liquid
(or **molten**) metal.

The **inner core** is the very centre of the
Earth. It is a huge ball of solid metal,
almost as hot as the surface of the sun!

In some special places, Earth's mantle melts. **Molten** rock is called **magma** and because it's lighter than solid rock, it rises up. Sometimes, magma bursts through the surface in a huge explosion, throwing out **ash** and rocky bits called **pumice** or **scoria**.

Other times, it flows out as **lava**, creating fiery rivers of molten rock. Over time, these **eruptions** can build up into volcanoes!

BUT WHY DOES THE MANTLE MELT?

The Earth's surface is divided up into huge pieces known as **tectonic plates**, which roughly fit together like the pieces of a giant jigsaw puzzle.

The plates move at just a few centimetres every year – about as slowly as your fingernails grow! Some of the plates lie under the oceans and others carry whole continents. Volcanoes often form at the edges of these plates. Where the plates pull apart or crash into each other, the temperature, pressure or chemical make-up of the **mantle** rock changes, so that it melts. Other volcanoes form in the middle of a plate, above special hotspots deep inside the Earth. That's how places like Hawaii were formed!

Sometimes, when two plates crash together, one sinks under the other creating volcanoes on the plate above.

When two plates pull apart this releases the pressure on the mantle underneath causing it to melt.

What different types of volcano are there?

When you think of a volcano, you probably picture a cone-shaped mountain spraying out fiery-coloured lava, but there are actually many different types of volcano . . .

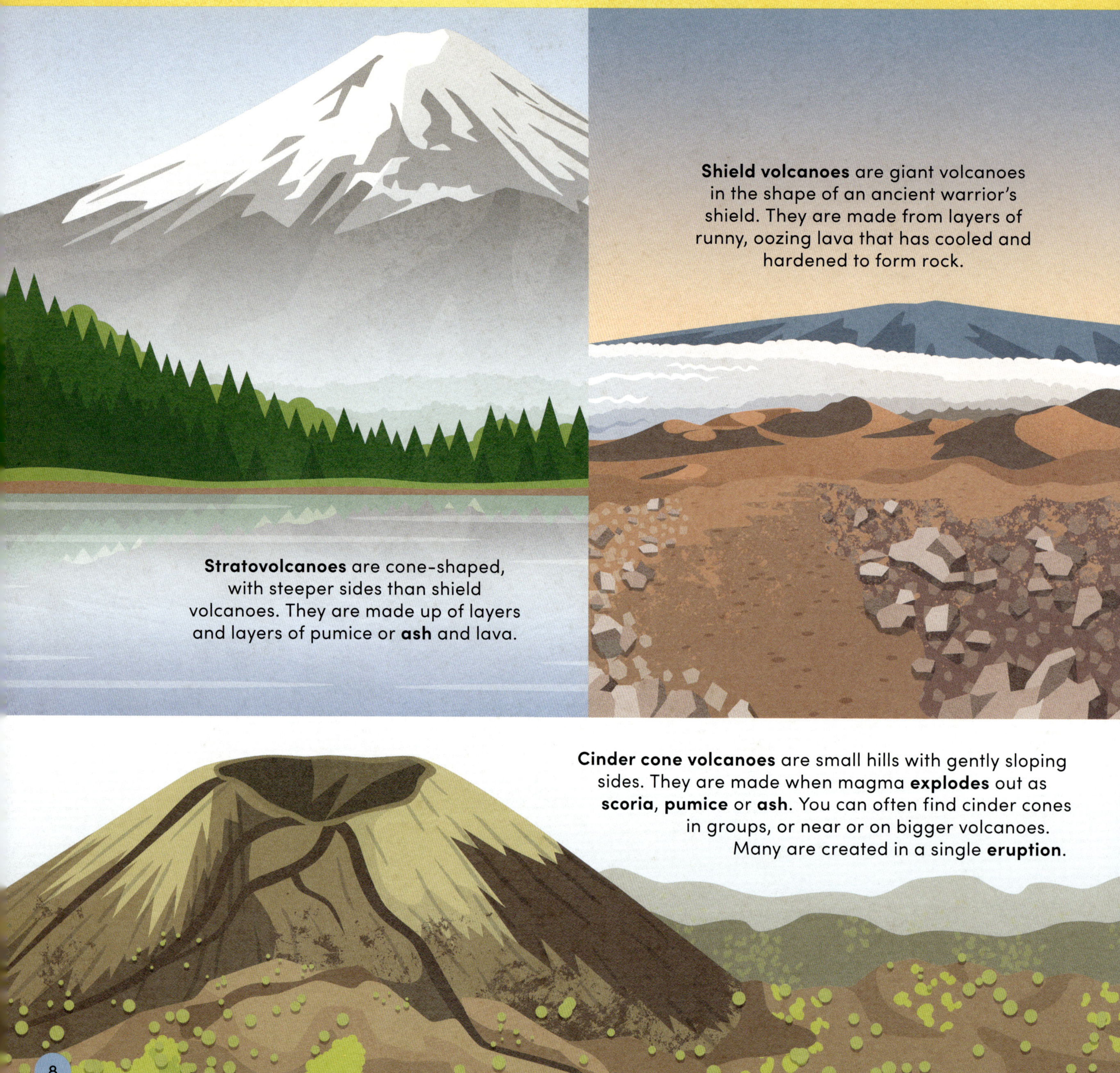

Shield volcanoes are giant volcanoes in the shape of an ancient warrior's shield. They are made from layers of runny, oozing lava that has cooled and hardened to form rock.

Stratovolcanoes are cone-shaped, with steeper sides than shield volcanoes. They are made up of layers and layers of pumice or **ash** and lava.

Cinder cone volcanoes are small hills with gently sloping sides. They are made when magma **explodes** out as **scoria**, **pumice** or **ash**. You can often find cinder cones in groups, or near or on bigger volcanoes. Many are created in a single **eruption**.

Some volcanic eruptions are so violent that they blow out a bowl-shaped hole called a **crater** or the force hollows out the shallow **crust** making it collapse under its own weight. The largest craters are called **calderas**, which means 'cauldron' or 'cooking pot' in Spanish.

Yellowstone in the USA is an example of a large caldera. It was formed in an eruption about 630,000 years ago, and it is so huge that it is easier to see from the air or from space than from the ground!

Yellowstone caldera is famous for its **hot springs**, **mudpots**, **fumaroles** and **geysers**. Old Faithful is the most famous geyser, and it erupts in a gushing steam plume every few hours.

Can you find volcanoes underwater?

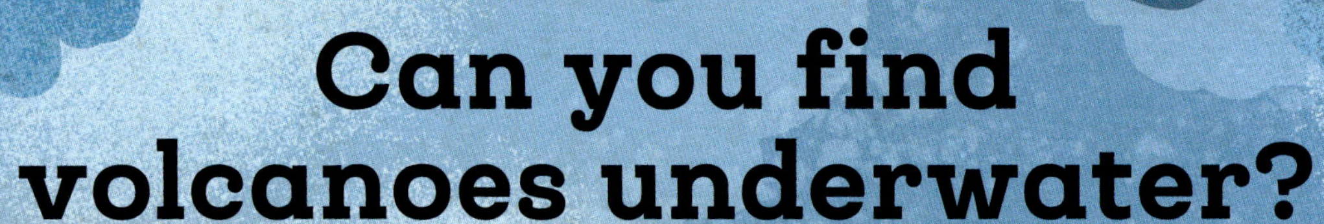

We might think of volcanoes as big mountains on land, but did you know that most volcanoes are actually hidden beneath the sea?

Most of these volcanoes can be found at the **mid-ocean ridges** where two **tectonic plates** are moving apart. Hot, runny (**basalt**) **lava** oozes up through cracks, quickly cooling in the water to form strange balloon-shaped rocks called **pillow lavas**.

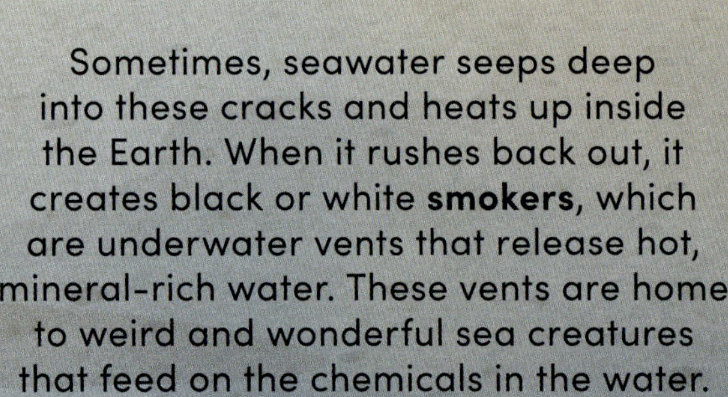

Sometimes, seawater seeps deep into these cracks and heats up inside the Earth. When it rushes back out, it creates black or white **smokers**, which are underwater vents that release hot, mineral-rich water. These vents are home to weird and wonderful sea creatures that feed on the chemicals in the water.

In some places where tectonic plates collide or in **mantle** hotspots, like Hawaii, underwater volcanoes erupt again and again for hundreds of thousands of years. Over time, they grow so large that they rise above the sea, forming their own islands.

One famous example is Surtsey, an island south of Iceland that appeared in the 1960s after a volcanic **eruption**.

GREAT WAVES

When volcanoes erupt under the sea, or when volcanic islands erupt, it can sometimes create enormous sea waves, known as **tsunamis**. The huge eruption of Krakatoa in Indonesia in 1883, caused a devastating tsunami, when the volcanic island collapsed into the sea.

In other places, volcanoes stay hidden beneath the waves and form underwater mountains called **seamounts**. Often, we only know when seamounts erupt because they produce huge rafts of floating **pumice** – a light, bubbly rock that floats on water.

Vent

Dike
(a fracture that magma can flow along)

Magma chamber
(where magma builds up before an eruption)

How does a volcano erupt?

Volcanoes can erupt in many different ways. Some gently bubble and ooze, while others explode with huge jets of rock and steam!

Deep inside the Earth, **magma** (the very hot melted rock) has lots of gas trapped inside, just like a bottle of fizzy lemonade. When the magma rises up, the pressure drops and the gas escapes.

EXPLOSIVE ERUPTIONS

If magma is sticky and full of gas, it traps bubbles inside. If the bubbles grow so big that they shatter the magma, the volcano explodes, shooting rocks, **ash** and **lava** into the sky – a bit like a shaken fizzy drink that explodes after you open the bottle!

PUMICE

The most powerful explosive eruptions are called **Plinian eruptions** – named after an ancient Roman man called Pliny, who described the explosion of Mount Vesuvius (see pages 14 and 15). They can send clouds of ash over 40 kilometres up into the air – that's higher than aeroplanes fly! The super-light, frothy rock from these eruptions is called **pumice** and it can float on water.

GENTLE, FLOWING VOLCANOES

If magma is runny, a type known as 'basaltic', it doesn't explode as violently. Sometimes it sprays into the air as a **fire fountain**, a few hundred metres high. This lava then cools into rocks called **scoria**. Once the **basalt** has lost its bubbles it can flow like a red-hot river of lava.

These lava flows can move as fast as a person walking and can travel for miles. You can see them in places like **Hawaii** or **Iceland**.

LOTS OF LAVA

Some lava is very thick and doesn't flow far. Instead, it piles up into steep mounds of rubble called **lava domes**. And sometimes, very rare eruptions make obsidian, a shiny black or dark green volcanic **glass** that people have used for making tools for thousands of years.

What happened at Pompeii and Herculaneum?

One of history's most well-known volcanic eruptions took place in Italy around 2,000 years ago . . .

Pompeii and Herculaneum were bustling, wealthy ancient Roman seaside cities on the idyllic coast of the Bay of Naples. They sat beneath a large mountain, covered in trees, where people would collect fresh water from mountain springs and hunt for wild animals. We now call this mountain Vesuvius and know that it is a volcano!

During the year of 79 CE, small earthquake shocks began underneath Vesuvius. Some wells and springs began to dry out, dead fish were found floating in the river, and grape vines wilted. But no one knew what was coming . . .

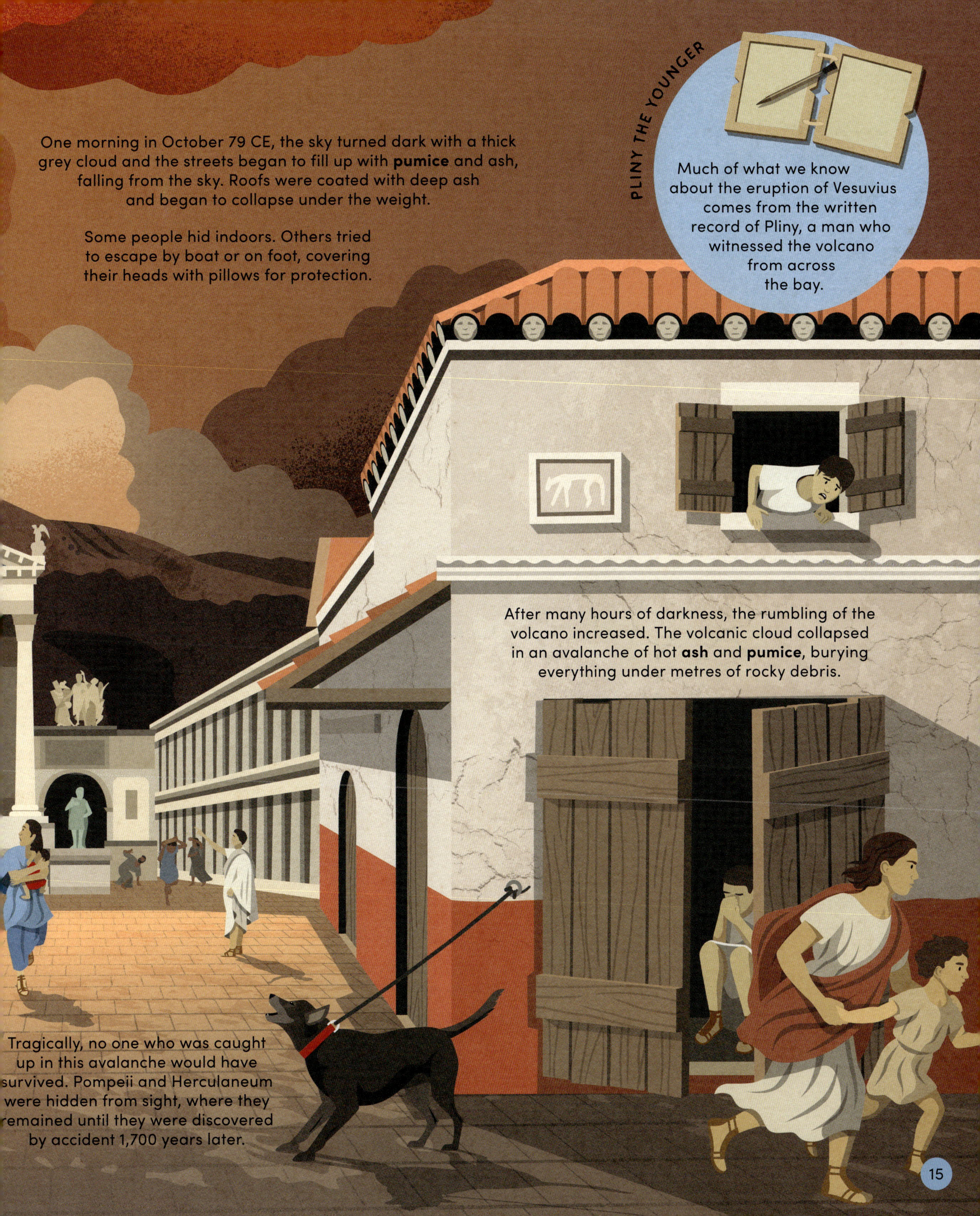

One morning in October 79 CE, the sky turned dark with a thick grey cloud and the streets began to fill up with **pumice** and ash, falling from the sky. Roofs were coated with deep ash and began to collapse under the weight.

Some people hid indoors. Others tried to escape by boat or on foot, covering their heads with pillows for protection.

Much of what we know about the eruption of Vesuvius comes from the written record of Pliny, a man who witnessed the volcano from across the bay.

After many hours of darkness, the rumbling of the volcano increased. The volcanic cloud collapsed in an avalanche of hot **ash** and **pumice**, burying everything under metres of rocky debris.

Tragically, no one who was caught up in this avalanche would have survived. Pompeii and Herculaneum were hidden from sight, where they remained until they were discovered by accident 1,700 years later.

How do scientists study volcanoes?

Scientists who study volcanoes are called volcanologists. It is not easy to explore these hot, magma-spewing places, so they wear protective clothing and carry special equipment.

A **helmet** protects their head from falling rock or ash.

A **gas mask** stops them breathing in harmful gases.

A **heatproof suit** keeps their body cool if they need to approach the lava.

Binoculars to help observe an eruption from a safe distance.

A **notebook** to make notes and sketches when collecting samples or making observations.

A **hand lens** is like a magnifying glass and helps them to see all the details in volcanic rock.

Thick boots are needed on the rough ground.

A **rock hammer** or drill can be used to collect chunks of rock as samples to be studied in a lab.

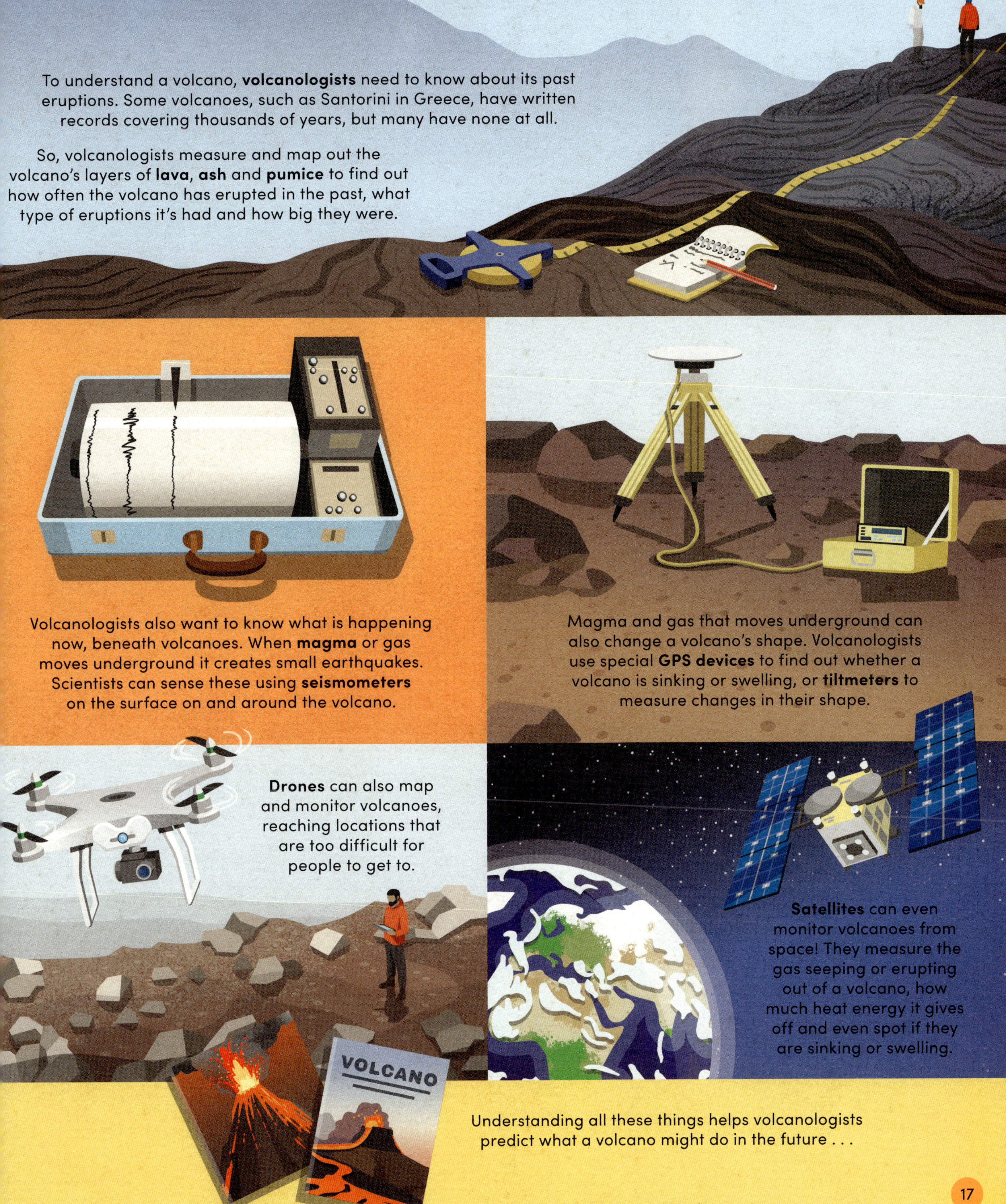

To understand a volcano, **volcanologists** need to know about its past eruptions. Some volcanoes, such as Santorini in Greece, have written records covering thousands of years, but many have none at all.

So, volcanologists measure and map out the volcano's layers of **lava**, **ash** and **pumice** to find out how often the volcano has erupted in the past, what type of eruptions it's had and how big they were.

Volcanologists also want to know what is happening now, beneath volcanoes. When **magma** or gas moves underground it creates small earthquakes. Scientists can sense these using **seismometers** on the surface on and around the volcano.

Magma and gas that moves underground can also change a volcano's shape. Volcanologists use special **GPS devices** to find out whether a volcano is sinking or swelling, or **tiltmeters** to measure changes in their shape.

Drones can also map and monitor volcanoes, reaching locations that are too difficult for people to get to.

Satellites can even monitor volcanoes from space! They measure the gas seeping or erupting out of a volcano, how much heat energy it gives off and even spot if they are sinking or swelling.

Understanding all these things helps volcanologists predict what a volcano might do in the future . . .

Can scientists predict eruptions?

Volcanologists have to be a bit like detectives, checking for clues to find out whether a volcano might erupt . . . and when.

Before an **eruption** starts, **magma** will rise up towards the surface. The movement of the magma will cause small earthquakes and make the ground bulge.

GPS DEVICES

THERMAL IMAGING CAMERA

Scientists might detect changes in the gases leaking out of the ground, or out of the volcano. Or they might see changes in the amount of heat coming out of the volcano.

DRONE

Sometimes scientists notice these changes long before the eruption, and they may be able to predict when and where an eruption might happen.

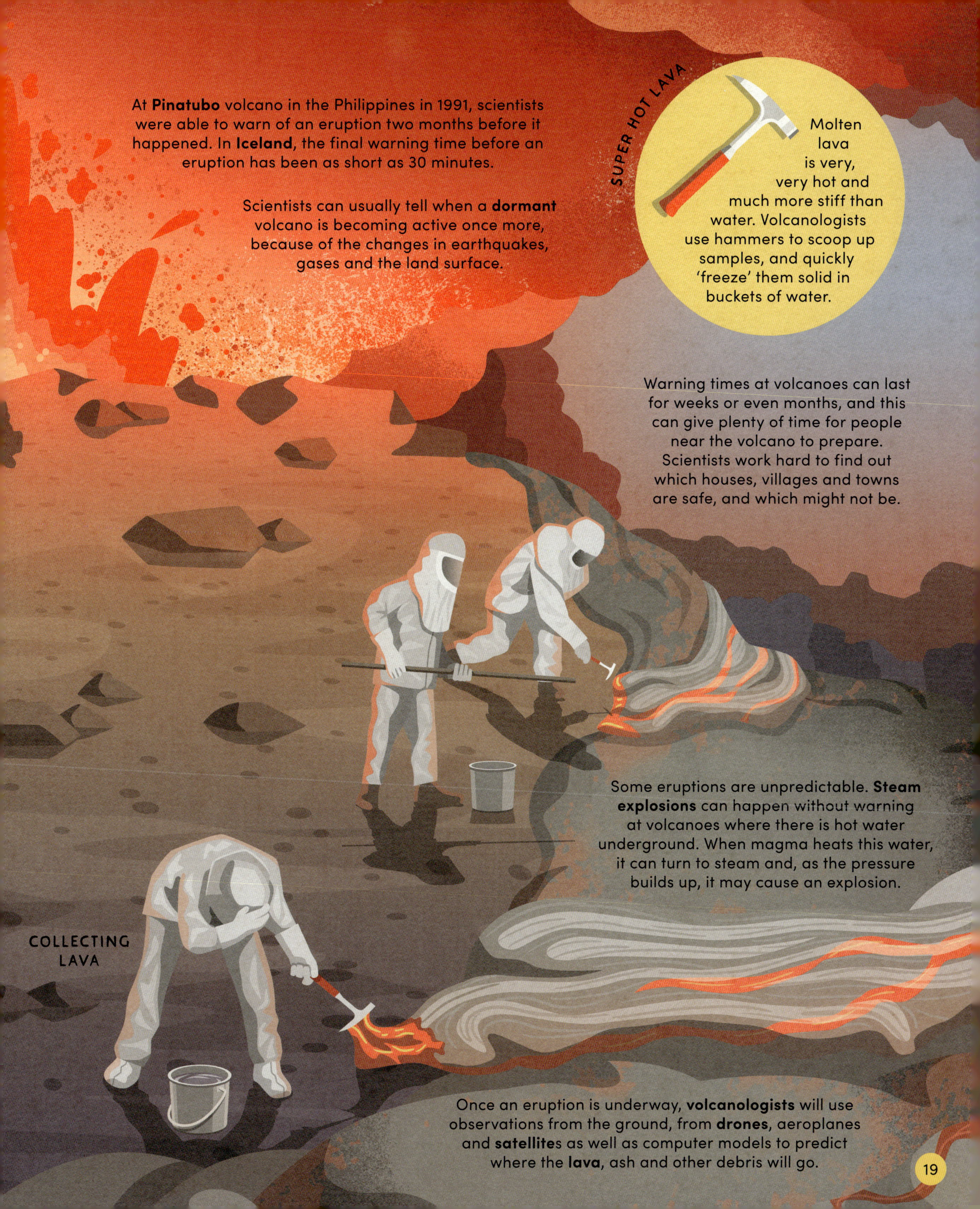

At **Pinatubo** volcano in the Philippines in 1991, scientists were able to warn of an eruption two months before it happened. In **Iceland**, the final warning time before an eruption has been as short as 30 minutes.

Scientists can usually tell when a **dormant** volcano is becoming active once more, because of the changes in earthquakes, gases and the land surface.

Molten lava is very, very hot and much more stiff than water. Volcanologists use hammers to scoop up samples, and quickly 'freeze' them solid in buckets of water.

Warning times at volcanoes can last for weeks or even months, and this can give plenty of time for people near the volcano to prepare. Scientists work hard to find out which houses, villages and towns are safe, and which might not be.

Some eruptions are unpredictable. **Steam explosions** can happen without warning at volcanoes where there is hot water underground. When magma heats this water, it can turn to steam and, as the pressure builds up, it may cause an explosion.

Once an eruption is underway, **volcanologists** will use observations from the ground, from **drones**, aeroplanes and **satellites** as well as computer models to predict where the **lava**, ash and other debris will go.

Can you live by a volcano?

Lots of people live near volcanoes! It is quite safe to live around volcanoes most of the time, and they can be great places to live . . .

The soil can be particularly good for growing crops.

Volcanic rocks can make excellent materials for building roads and houses.

Many volcanic mountains have reliable water supplies.

Many volcanoes contain precious metals and **minerals**, including **copper**, **silver** and **gold**.

Lots of tourists visit volcanoes, which brings money to the people who live there.

We can also get **geothermal energy** to make electricity from volcanoes.

Some of the heat from inside the Earth leaks out around volcanoes. This heat can be used as a renewable energy source, which means it does not run out like oil, coal and gas.

Some animals choose to live on or near volcanoes, too . . .

Lesser flamingos travel to Lake Natron, near Ol Doinyo Lengai volcano in Tanzania, to breed and feed. The hot, chemical-filled water there is harmful to most other animals.

Japanese macaques love to bathe in the **hot springs** of Japan's volcanic hills during the chilly winter months.

Volcanic **crater** lakes can be places where animals thrive. One ancient crater lake in Cameroon contains twelve unique species of fish.

Female Galápagos land iguanas climb all the way to the top of La Cumbre volcano to lay their eggs. The temperature in the volcano's crater is just right for their young to hatch.

But volcanic eruptions can deeply change people's way of life even if they are kept safe.

The **Soufrière Hills volcano**, on the Caribbean island of Montserrat, had not erupted for at least 400 years. In July 1995, a small eruption began with very little warning. Over the next few months, volcanic explosions made it too risky to stay nearby. Within two years, more than half of the people on the island had left. Today, plants and trees are starting to grow back and tourists visit to see the volcano.

Why do we get different types of volcanic rocks?

On our planet, there are three main types of rock: sedimentary, metamorphic and igneous. Igneous rock is made when magma cools and hardens.

There are many different types of **igneous rock**. They look different depending on what **minerals** and bubbles they contain and how glassy the rocks are. The type you get depends on the **magma**'s journey as it passes through the Earth's **mantle** and **crust**.

HUGE HEXAGONS

Sometimes when magma cools, it fractures into hexagonal columns. These form famous landscapes like Giant's Causeway in Northern Ireland and Devils Tower in Wyoming, USA.

Basalt is the most common type of igneous rock. This is what the ocean floor is made of. The magma it comes from flows easily, like runny honey. When it cools on the surface, it forms a strong, dark grey or black **lava** with small crystals.

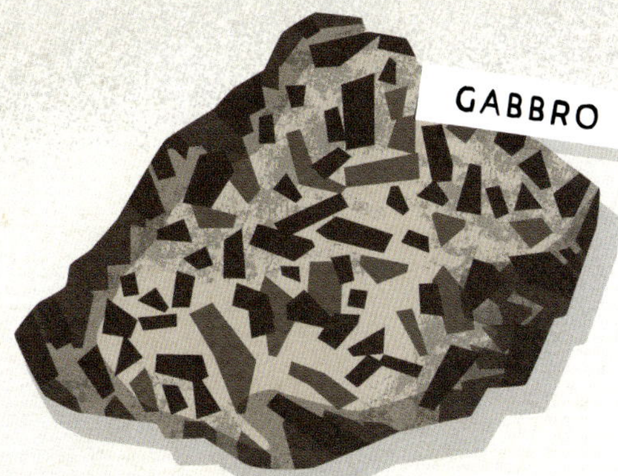

GABBRO

When liquid basalt magma cools and becomes a solid very slowly inside the Earth, it turns into a rock called **gabbro** that is made up of larger crystals.

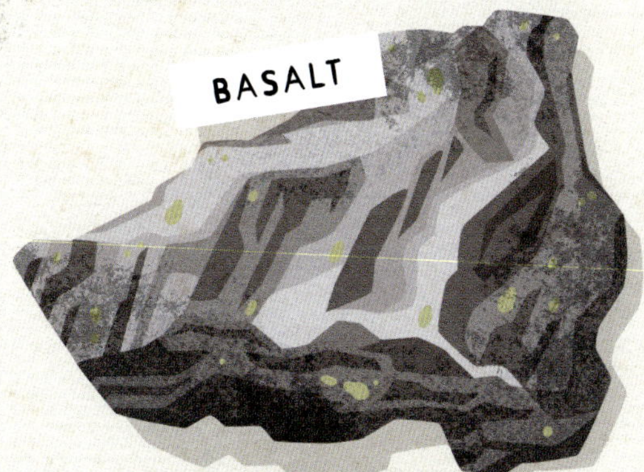

BASALT

ANDESITE

Andesite is usually a grey or light-coloured rock. The magma that creates andesite is much stickier than basalt, and usually erupts explosively from a volcano or forms thick **lava** flows or domes. It can build steep **stratovolcano**es.

RHYOLITE

Rhyolite is also usually light in colour. Like magma, it is very sticky and can sometimes forms glassy obsidian flows. More often, it explodes to form **ash** and **pumice**. When it freezes inside the Earth, it forms **granite**.

PUMICE

Granite is a hard, speckled rock, made of different-coloured larger crystals. It is used to make floors, kitchen countertops and monuments!

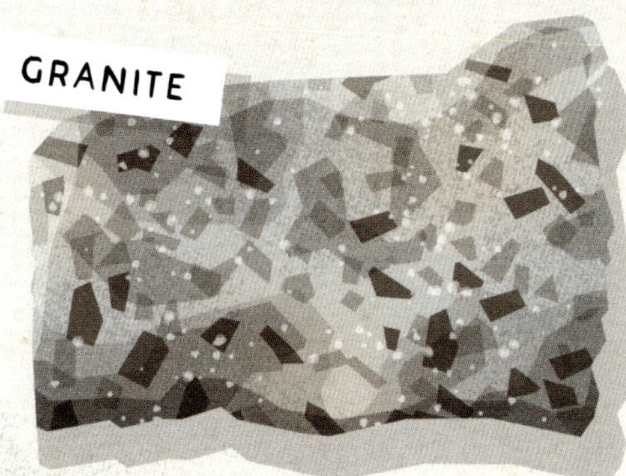

GRANITE

Pumice is a pale-coloured rock. It forms when magma cools very quickly, preserving the bubbles inside the frothing rock as it erupts. This makes it so light that it can float on water. People sometimes use it to scrub away rough skin on their feet!

What are the biggest volcanoes and eruptions on Earth?

We have explored many different types of volcanoes and eruptions, from underwater vents to fire-fountains to city-burying eruptions. But how big can they get?

Hawaii's **Mauna Loa** is the largest active volcano on our planet. It rises more than four kilometres above sea level and descends five kilometres below the waves to the seafloor. In fact, it is so heavy that the Pacific plate sags at least another five kilometres below it like a hammock. From its roots to its tip, Mauna Loa is more than one and a half times taller than Mount Everest!

The eruption of **Mount Tambora** volcano in Indonesia in April 1815 is the largest known explosive eruption of the last 500 years. Tambora erupted over 100 cubic kilometres of rock and killed at least 71,000 people. One cubic kilometre of **pumice** and **ash** would form a layer 70 cm thick, across the whole of London.

But we know from studying volcanoes that there have been much larger eruptions in the past . . .

Some eruptions throw out more than 1,000 cubic kilometres of rock. These eruptions are sometimes called **supereruptions**. Thankfully, they are very rare. The last one was the Oruanui eruption of Taupo volcano, New Zealand, about 26,500 years ago.

Other famous examples are colossal eruptions from volcanoes such as **Yellowstone** in the USA or **Toba** in Indonesia.

There have been about 20 supereruptions in the last 15 million years. They leave behind huge **calderas** and vast quantities of ash, pumice and other volcanic debris.

The largest volcanic events in Earth's history are known as **large igneous provinces**. These last about a million years and erupt about a million cubic kilometres of **lava**. They leave huge areas covered in stacks of lava flows in places like the **Deccan traps** in India, and the **Emeishan** in China.

The most recent large igneous province is the Columbia River in the USA, which erupted about 16 million years ago. These events have been linked to mass extinctions and times of major environmental change in our planet's history.

How do volcanoes change our climate?

We have seen how volcanoes can devastate local places when they erupt, but did you know that eruptions can also change climate and weather patterns around the world?

The summer of 1816 was really cold across the northeast USA, Canada and western Europe. Crops failed and there were many food shortages. In Switzerland, some people were so hungry they had to eat moss. At the time, no one could explain what had caused this strange weather. But scientists now believe it was all because of the huge 1815 eruption of **Mount Tambora** in Indonesia.

Our planet is wrapped in a layer of gases called the **atmosphere**. The atmosphere gives us the air we breathe, and we can feel these gases moving when it is windy.

The atmosphere also protects Earth from some of the harmful parts of the Sun's rays and keeps enough heat in that we do not freeze.

Large volcanic eruptions can push a gas called **sulphur dioxide** high into the atmosphere, where it reacts and forms a **haze** of acid **droplets**, covering a large area. The small droplets reflect some of the Sun's energy back out into space. This cools the Earth's surface and disturbs weather patterns.

It takes a few years for the gas and haze to disappear and things to return to normal. The haze in the upper atmosphere can also lead to very spectacular sunsets after big volcanic eruptions.

Some people have suggested that after a **supereruption** Earth might experience a **volcanic winter** lasting up to 10 years! Thankfully, supereruptions are very, very rare.

Other volcanic gases like **carbon dioxide** help to keep our planet warm. A single big eruption contains only a small amount of carbon dioxide compared to what's already in the atmosphere, but if we switched off all the world's volcanoes, over time our planet would get colder.

Are there volcanoes in space?

Many of the planets and moons in our Solar System have volcanoes, too. Some of these other worlds haven't seen eruptions for billions of years, but others are still active.

Have you ever noticed dark patches on the Moon? These are known as **maria**, and they are the result of ancient volcanoes! Most of the Moon's volcanoes erupted three to four billion years ago and all of them are now long dead.

We can also see volcanoes on Mars using telescopes and, more recently, **orbiters**. Mars has the largest volcano in the Solar System, Olympus Mons. It towers 25 kilometres above its surroundings (almost three times the height of Mount Everest), with a footprint the size of France. Today, though, there is no sign of significant active volcanoes on Mars.

Radar images show many volcanic features, and perhaps even active volcanoes, on Venus. But Venus is very, very hot and covered in cloud, so it is hard to study. Hopefully future space missions will teach us more.

The most volcanically active world in the Solar System is Io, one of **Jupiter's** moons. In 1979, the **Voyager 1** space probe sent back images of Io showing a gigantic umbrella-shaped fountain spurting from the moon's surface. This was the first evidence of a volcanic eruption on another planet!

Some space volcanoes spew out ice and water instead of hot lava! They are called **cryovolcanoes** and can be found on Europa, a moon of Jupiter, Enceladus, a moon of Saturn, and Triton, a moon of Neptune.

IT IS CLEAR THAT VOLCANOES ARE IMPORTANT FAR BEYOND EARTH. THERE IS STILL MUCH WE DON'T KNOW ABOUT SPACE VOLCANOES – MAYBE ONE DAY YOU WILL HELP TO DISCOVER MORE OF THEIR SECRETS.

Glossary

Ash

A mixture of rock, mineral and glass fragments erupted from a volcano.

Basalt

A dark-coloured lava erupted from a volcano, that turns into a rock when it cools on the Earth's surface.

Caldera

A very large crater in the ground that is made by a very big volcanic eruption.

Crater

A bowl-shaped hole in the ground that can be caused by volcanic eruptions.

Crust

Earth's rocky outer layer, which forms the ocean floors and the land we walk on.

Dormant

Describes a volcano that has not erupted for some time but could erupt again in the future.

Drone

A flying machine that can travel without a human on board. Drones help monitor volcanoes which are too difficult or dangerous for people to reach.

Eruption

The release of melted rock, ash and gases from a volcano. These releases can sometimes be explosive but other times flow more gently.

Fumarole

A small hole or crack in the ground that releases volcanic gases.

Geothermal energy

Heat that is tapped from beneath the Earth's surface. It can be used for things like warming buildings or generating electricity.

Geyser

A type of hot spring that sometimes appears in volcanic areas. It intermittently shoots hot water and steam into the air.

GPS device

A device that uses satellite signals to detect tiny movements of the Earth's surface. It can help scientists to monitor volcanoes.

Hot spring

A pool of hot water produced from rain or other water, volcanic heat and gases.

Igneous rock

A type of rock that is formed when magma cools and hardens.

Lava

Very hot, melted rock that comes out of erupting volcanoes.

Magma

Hot, melted rock that is usually found under the Earth's surface but can sometimes burst through it as lava.

Mantle

The largest of Earth's layers. It lies below Earth's crust and is made up of very hot, slow-moving rock.

Mid-ocean ridges

A long, underwater mountain chain deep on the ocean floor formed where tectonic plates pull apart. Most of the Earth's volcanic activity happens here.

Minerals

Naturally occurring substances that make up rocks, sand and soil on the Earth. Sometimes they look like crystals.

Molten

Describes when a material (like rock or metal) is melted by a very high heat.

Mudpot

A pool of hot, bubbling mud produced by volcanic heat and gases and rain or other water.

Orbiter

A spacecraft that travels around a planet or moon collecting images and data, including details about its volcanic activity.

Pumice

A very light rock that is full of tiny holes. It forms when magma from an exploding volcano cools very quickly.

Radar image

A picture that uses invisible radio waves to detect and monitor faraway objects, such as volcanoes in space!

Satellite

A machine that orbits a planet. Some satellites monitor Earth from space. Some can track important things about volcanoes like how they move or how much heat energy or gas they give out.

Scoria

A dark-coloured, bubbly rock made from lava that has cooled.

Seamount

An underwater mountain that rises from the sea floor. Usually, seamounts are remnants of extinct volcanoes, but some seamounts still erupt.

Seismometer

A tool that can measure shaking in the ground caused by events like earthquakes and volcanic eruptions.

Stratovolcano

A steep, cone-shaped volcano that is formed by layers of hardened lava and ash.

Supereruption

Huge and rare volcanic eruptions that throw out more than 1000 cubic kilometres of rock.

Tectonic plates

Large, shifting pieces of rock that make up Earth's outer layer. Their movements can cause volcanoes to form or erupt.

Thermal imaging camera

A special device that detects heat energy. It can be used to help scientists monitor volcanic eruptions.

Tiltmeter

A tool that measures changes in the tilt of the Earth's surface and can help to track the shape of volcanoes.

Tsunami

A huge and powerful ocean wave which can be caused by a violent volcanic eruption.

Volcanic winter

When the Earth's climate becomes colder after a gigantic volcanic eruption. This cooling happens because large amounts of gas from the volcano make a haze in Earth's upper atmosphere blocking out the sun's warmth.

Volcanologist

A scientist who studies volcanoes, monitoring important things like how and why they form and erupt.

Index